# EJ's Exciting Road Trip

By:  Edwin Bonilla, Jr. and Suze Guillaume

Illustrated by: Abira Das

From Selma, Alabama 50th Anniversary of Bloody Sunday to the White House in Washington, D.C.

Build and Inspire, LLC

Printed in the United States of America

First Printing, 2015

ISBN-13 978-0-9961161-0-7

Build & Inspire, LLC

P.O. Box 681664

Miami, FL 33168

www.suzeguillaume.com

This little light of mine,

I'm going to let it shine.

EJ woke up very early on his fifth birthday. He was excited about what his family had planned for him. He wasn't going to have a regular old birthday party like everyone else. After months of waiting, EJ and his family were finally going to the White House! When he was just four years old, EJ asked his mom to visit the White House. Now, on his fifth birthday, his dream was coming true! EJ was so eager to visit the White House that he told all of his friends at school about his exciting trip.

The road to the White House was far away and EJ was ready to get there. He knew the White House had the United States flag on the roof. He also knew the president lived there with his family, but he did not know what was on the inside. Did the White House have a kitchen and living room like EJ's house? In just a day or two, EJ would find out!

The family was ready to travel, but EJ was missing something. He had his baseball, backpack, blanket, and toys. What was he missing? Oh no! EJ forgot his United States flag! Just before his mom could lock the door to their house, EJ rushed back to his room to get his flag. Boy, was that a close one! After getting his flag, he hopped into the back seat of the car, and off they went on an exciting road trip.

The road to the White House was far away, and EJ thought they would never get there. As time passed, he continued to ask his mom "Are we there yet?" and his mom always replied, "No, we are still miles away." EJ could not understand why it was taking so long to get to the White House.

Night time came and went, and **EJ** continued to play with his toys, but he was still very anxious. He asked so many questions until he got so tired and fell asleep.

Welcome to
Sweet Home
Alabama

After a full day on the road, EJ woke up and looked around to see if they had finally made it to the White House. He saw many colorful trees and leaves near a sign that read "Welcome to Sweet Home Alabama". EJ knew the White House was not in Alabama, so he asked his mom, "Why are we in Alabama?" His mom explained, "We are here to visit a historical site." EJ was confused. He didn't know what a historical site was, but he was excited because his mom said that the site had a very huge bridge that he could run across.

As the family got close to the bridge, EJ saw lots of people. He asked why are so many people visiting the bridge. His mom explained, "So many people had to cross this bridge to help unite the country.  Today, Selma, Alabama is celebrating the 50th anniversary of the March from Selma to Montgomery. Activists organized a march for voting rights." EJ was still a bit confused, but when he looked ahead he was happy to be there.

EDMUND PETTUS BRIDG

There were kids and their families everywhere. EJ was a part of history and he felt proud! As EJ was crossing the bridge with his family, he saw the Alabama River. After crossing the bridge with so many people, it was getting really cold and the sun was setting. EJ knew it was time to head back to the car. He asked his mom if they were heading to the White House. His mom said that they would have to rest first.

The next day EJ and his family arrived at the Civil Rights Institute in Birmingham, Alabama. When they got there, EJ saw a huge church across the street with many stairs. He saw a sign that read "16th Street Baptist Church". EJ's mom told him that Dr. Martin Luther King, Jr. went to the church when he was younger to gather people to stand up for equality. EJ knew that Dr. Martin Luther King, Jr. was a great person.

This was EJ's first time visiting a museum where he would learn about equal opportunity. He saw segregated water fountains and classrooms. He even saw a statue of Rosa Parks. EJ asked his mom why Rosa Parks looked so sad. His mom said that Rosa Parks was asked to move out of her seat on a bus so a white person could sit down. When she refused to move to the back of the bus, she was thrown in jail. EJ got closer to Rosa Parks and touched the statue. He felt bad because she looked so sad. As EJ continued to walk around the museum, he saw a bus that had been set on fire. He was surprised and knew something went wrong. His mom told him that the bus boycotts began thanks to Rosa Parks and her bravery.

EJ and his family entered another part of the museum where they saw a jail cell with a mattress on the floor. EJ learned that Dr. Martin Luther King, Jr. stayed in that cell. EJ could not believe that Dr. Martin Luther King, Jr. was taken to jail for helping people. He thought only bad people had to go to jail. EJ's mom explained to him that protesting was illegal when Dr. Martin Luther King, Jr. was alive. Back then, people had to protest sometimes because the state of Alabama and other states were segregated. EJ learned that segregation meant black people and white people could not visit the same areas or shop in the same stores. He also learned that Dr. Martin Luther King, Jr. was a good man who believed in equal opportunity for all people, and he would not let anything get in the way of that.

After leaving the museum, EJ saw a statue of a very tall man. It was Fred Shuttlesworth. His family told him that Fred Shuttlesworth was a Baptist minister who was one of the top leaders of the Civil Rights Movement working with Dr. Martin Luther King, Jr. EJ took a picture of the statue and told his family that he will remember anyone that worked with Dr. Martin Luther King, Jr.

After several days on the road, EJ and his family
arrived to Washinghton, D.C., and EJ was excited!
He saw tall buildings and a busy city. The family had
finally made it to the White House! At the visitor's
entrance, EJ saw a long line of people waiting to go
on the famous White House Tour. He even saw
special men in black suits standing all around.
EJ remembered seeing them on television with the
president, but he thought they were just friends with
the president. EJ's family explained that the men in
the black suits were Secret Service officers who
helped protect the president and the White House.

While they waited in line, EJ heard a loud sound.
He asked one of the Secret Service officers if he
knew what was making the sound. The officer told
EJ it was his favorite person, President Barack
Obama. The president was leaving on a helicopter to
take care of business. EJ waved as high as he could
to tell the president farewell.

Finally, after what seemed like forever, EJ had a Secret Service officer who welcomed him to the White House and took him and his family to the front of the line for a private tour. EJ was so happy. He held his United States flag tightly as he entered the White House. Although EJ had a private tour, he and his family still had to wait to get checked in by the Secret Service officers. EJ asked, "Why do they have to check everyone?" His mom replied, "They have to make sure our names match what is on their list. They also have to make sure we do not carry in items that are not allowed in the White House."

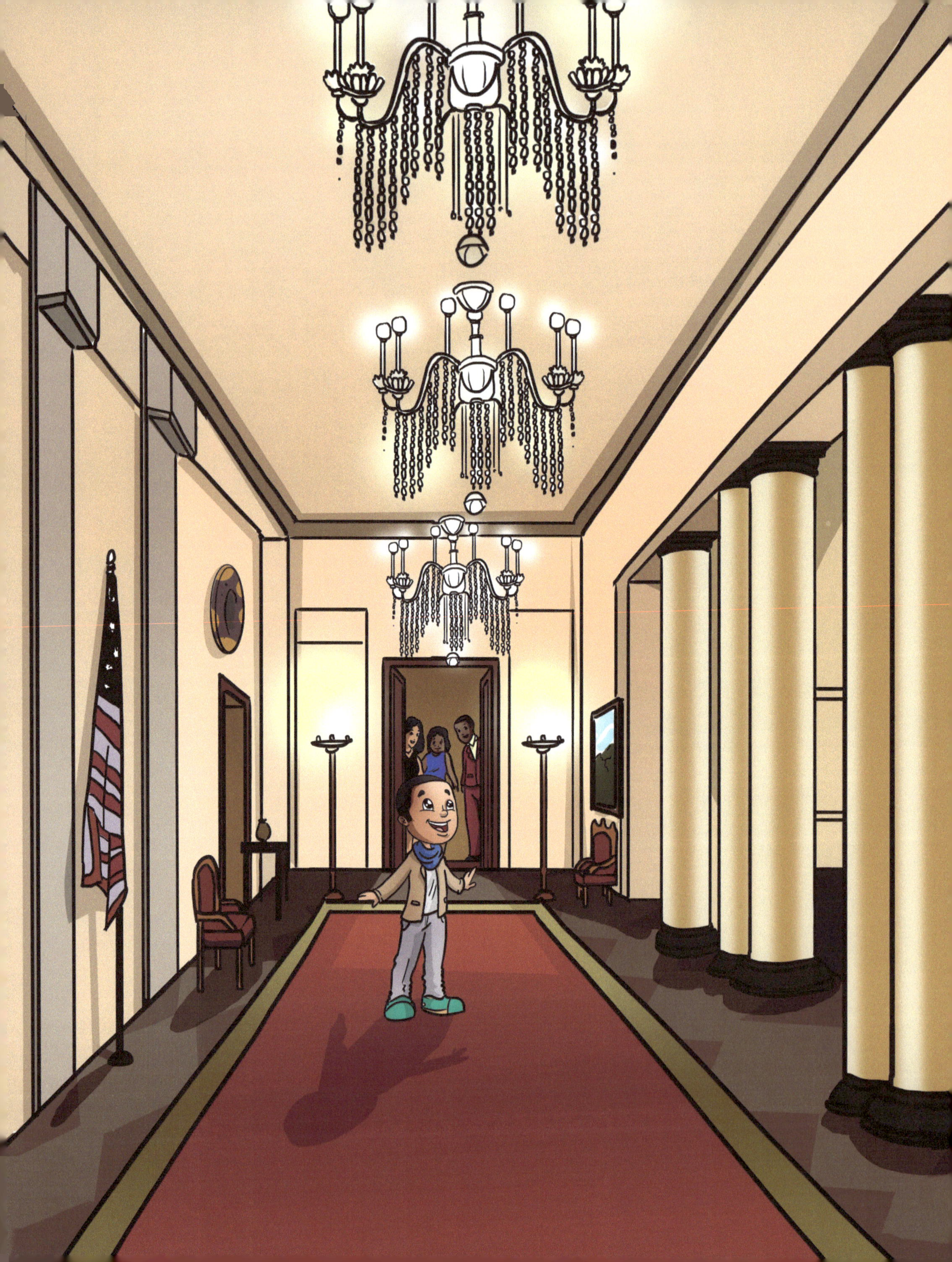

EJ and his family made it into the White House. As EJ was running through the hallways, he saw pictures of all the presidents from the past. His family was happy for him. His birthday wish was granted.

EJ entered the Center Hall where the floors were bright and gleaming clean just like he imagined. When he ran into the White House Library, he was told not to enter. This made EJ a bit upset because he thought that he could go into all of the rooms. The Secret Service officer explained that the White House Library was closed for a special event. This made EJ even more curious, but he followed directions and stayed out of the library.

EJ continued to walk with his mom to the next floor where they saw several more rooms. The first room he saw was the East Room. EJ learned that the East Room is the largest room in the White House. The president currently uses it for press conferences.

The next room EJ saw was the Blue Room which serves as the formal reception area for guests of the president. There was a picture of George Washington that EJ recognized.

The next room EJ saw was the Green Room. The tour guide told EJ that this room is more like a relaxing room. The colors of the different rooms made them easy to remember.

The Red Room was a bright red room and it stood out. It is used for formal and informal events. EJ was able to walk into the room with his family. He told his mom that he wanted a room as bright as the Red Room.

The State Dining Room is a famous room where special people meet with the president. EJ imagined himself sitting at the dining table eating dinner with President Barack Obama and his family. Boy, what a treat that would be!

As EJ got closer to the exit he saw a statue head of a president. He was proud to tell his family that the statue was of Abraham Lincoln. EJ even pulled out a $5.00 bill just to show everyone how much he really knew about the presidents.

As EJ was leaving the White House, he told the
Secret Service officer that he would return soon.
The officer asked if he would return as the president.
With a big smile on his face, EJ answered, "Yes, I
will return as president!"

As EJ and his family walked out of the White House, EJ gave his mom a big hug and told her thanks for taking him to the White House. Just before they got back into their car, EJ held up his United States flag as high as he could and pointed it towards the flag on top of the White House. Not only was EJ proud to be an American, he was also proud to be the future president of the United States of America.

# The End

Photo Credit: Innovative Arts By Tracy Ann

Special Thanks

I would first like to thank my Father in Heaven for giving my son the vision to write his story with my guidance. We would like to thank Marlon "Uncle Marlon" Hill for granting my son's birthday wish to visit the White House. Special thanks to our friends and family who believed in this project. We are grateful for all of you. We will continue to write more stories to empower children all over the world.

To schedule a White House Tour for your family, please visit https://www.whitehouse.gov/participate/tours-and-events

All things are possible with God!